MIND-BLOWING SCIENCE EXPERIMENTS

AWESOME EXPERIMENTS WITH

LIVING THINGS

Thomas Canavan

Gareth Stevens
PUBLISHING

Please visit our website, www.garethstevens.com.
For a free color catalog of all our high-quality books,
call toll free 1-800-542-2595 or fax 1-877-542-2596.

Cataloging-in-Publication Data

Names: Canavan, Thomas.
Title: Awesome experiments with living things / Thomas Canavan.
Description: New York : Gareth Stevens Publishing, 2018. I Series: Mind-blowing science experiments I Includes index.
Identifiers: ISBN 9781538207468 (pbk.) I ISBN 9781538207406 (library bound) I ISBN 9781538207284 (6 pack)
Subjects: LCSH: Plants--Experiments--Juvenile literature.
Classification: LCC QK52.6 C317 2018 I DDC 580.78--dc23

Published in 2018 by
Gareth Stevens Publishing
111 East 14th Street, Suite 349
New York, NY 10003

Author: Thomas Canavan
Illustrator: Adam Linley
Experiments Coordinator: Anna Middleton
Designer: Elaine Wilkinson
Designer series edition: Emma Randall
Editors: Joe Harris, Rebecca Clunes, Frances Evans

All images courtesy of Shutterstock.

Printed in China

CPSIA compliance information: Batch CS17GS: For further information contact
Gareth Stevens, New York, New York at 1-800-542-2595.

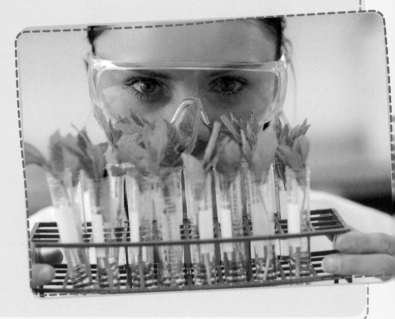

Having Fun and Being Safe

Inside this book you'll find a whole range of exciting science experiments that can be performed safely at home. Nearly all the equipment you need will be found around your own house. Anything that you don't have at home should be available at a local store.

We have given some recommendations alongside the instructions to let you know when adult help might be needed. However, the degree of adult supervision will vary, depending on the age of the reader and the experiment. We would recommend close adult supervision for any experiment involving cooking equipment, sharp implements, electrical equipment, or batteries.

The author and publisher cannot take responsibility for any injury, damage, or mess that might occur as a result of attempting the experiments in this book. Always tell an adult before you perform any experiments, and follow the instructions carefully.

Contents

A note about measurements

Measurements are given in U.S. form with metric in parentheses. The metric conversion is rounded to make it easier to measure.

You can play detective as you explore the science behind living things and how they grow—you'll even use fingerprints! You and your friends will also get to be the "living things" in some experiments!

the Damp Drumbeat

Some experiments boil down to having fun! Learning how plants get their water is much funnier than you'd think! Follow these steps to find out for yourself.

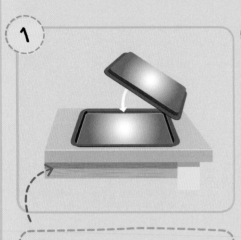

1

Set the larger baking tray on a table or counter, and the smaller one upside down on it. This placement will help with sound effects later.

2

Put a handful of the dried peas in the jar and place the jar in the center of the smaller baking tray.

3

Carefully fill the jar to the top with cold water.

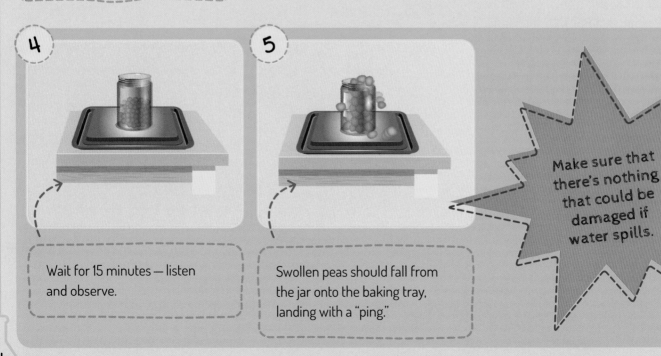

4

Wait for 15 minutes — listen and observe.

5

Swollen peas should fall from the jar onto the baking tray, landing with a "ping."

Make sure that there's nothing that could be damaged if water spills.

HOW DOES IT WORK?

This experiment is all about the way water moves through the **cells** of plants and animals. This process is called osmosis, and it's what happens when you put a dry sponge in water. The sponge draws in water until it's as wet as the water around it. That's what happened to the peas. As they absorbed water, they swelled up. They began to take up more space, gradually filling up the jar and falling out, one by one. Your double-tray arrangement made it easier to hear each pea falling out.

TOP TIP!

Most types of dried peas will work in this experiment, but the best results come from ordinary garden peas that have been sold dried.

WHAT HAPPENS IF...?

Try doing the same experiment with fresh peas instead of dried peas. If they're not in season, drain some peas from a can and use those. How long will you have to wait until they start making that "ping" sound, one by one? Make a **prediction** and test it.

REAL-LIFE SCIENCE

Osmosis is a form of passive transport. Active transport is different—it needs **energy** to work. Just think of how your heart pumps blood through your body. Passive transport relies instead on the basic chemical process of osmosis. The tissue of plants and animals allows water to pass through in each direction, helping to supply **nutrients** and take away waste.

Testing For Prints

YOU WILL NEED

- Baby powder (or corn flour)
- Clear tape
- Black card stock
- Hand lotion
- Small paintbrush or makeup brush
- Magnifying glass (optional)

Every time you watch a crime show on TV, you probably hear the phrase "Test it for prints." But how are fingerprints left behind, and what do they look like? Solve these mysteries with this experiment!

1

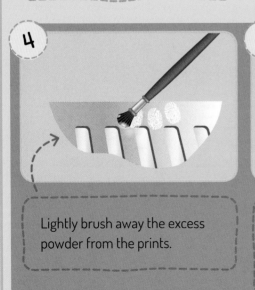

Rub a small amount of lotion on your hands, concentrating on your fingertips. Find a smooth surface area, such as a countertop or the edge of a sink.

2

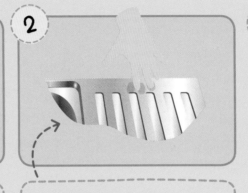

Press two or three fingers down on that surface. You'll leave behind fingerprints.

3

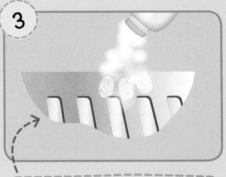

Sprinkle a little bit of powder on the surface where you have left the fingerprints. You should be able to see them better.

4

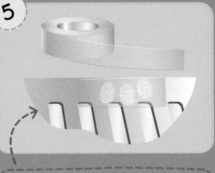

Lightly brush away the excess powder from the prints.

5

Carefully stretch a piece of tape over the prints and press down on the surface.

6

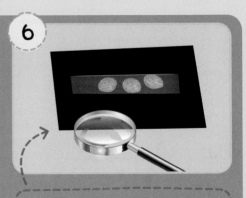

Lift the tape and carefully press it onto the black card stock. You can use a magnifying glass to look at the prints closely!

HOW DOES IT WORK?

Your skin constantly produces oils to keep itself from drying out. Some of this oil is left behind when you touch anything, but it's hard to trace on many surfaces such as rough wood or cotton. Fingers do leave a clear trace behind, though, on smooth surfaces. In step 1 of the experiment, you enhanced this effect by using lotion. The raised, swirly ridges on your fingertips leave a pattern behind—fingerprints.

Normally, you wouldn't notice fingerprints, but "dusting" with powder makes them stand out. By transferring prints—like you did with clear tape—scientists can study the evidence far from "the scene of the crime."

TOP TIP!

Press firmly but gently when you leave the prints.

REAL-LIFE SCIENCE

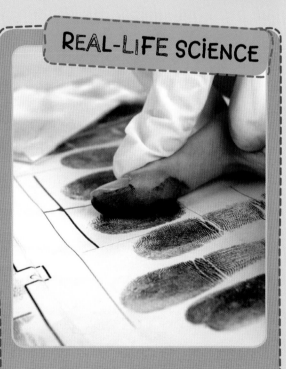

Fingerprints are especially important because no two people have the same pattern of ridges on the surface of their fingertips. That means that everyone's fingerprints are **unique**. Detectives can match fingerprint evidence with suspects' prints to see whether there's a link to a crime scene.

WHAT HAPPENS IF...?

Of course, knowing how to leave and test for prints is only half the fun. You could mark a section of paper and have your friends each press a finger into some ink. Then they could press their finger onto the paper. With each person's prints recorded, you could really begin to play detective by trying to identify whose prints are on the counter!

Feel the Burn

YOU WILL NEED

- Clothespin
- Watch or timer

You've probably heard people talking about how important it is to "feel the burn" when they're working out in the gym. But what "burning" are they talking about? Is there a way to find out without getting burned for real? Yes—with this experiment!

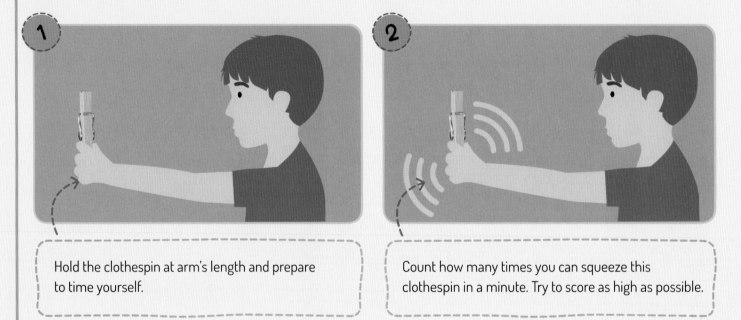

1 Hold the clothespin at arm's length and prepare to time yourself.

2 Count how many times you can squeeze this clothespin in a minute. Try to score as high as possible.

3 Continue counting until the minute is up, or the "burn" gets a little too extreme.

Remember, this should be fun! Stop if your hand hurts or if you feel a cramp developing.

HOW DOES IT WORK?

As you can see, this is one of the simplest and quickest experiments you can do. But it demonstrates something very important, even more important than working up a sweat at the local gym! Your muscles need **oxygen** for energy and when you exercise fast enough, they need more than the oxygen carried by your blood. Muscles then use glucose (a type of sugar) to produce energy. Lactic acid is produced in this reaction. If lactic acid builds up—and can't be sent away quickly enough—you start to feel a burning sensation.

TOP TIP!

Don't worry if you stop before the minute is up—you'll probably start feeling the burn by then anyway!

REAL-LIFE SCIENCE

Energy can be measured in **calories**. People can lose weight by reducing the amount of calories in their diet or by burning them through exercise. "Feeling the burn" is a sign that lots of calories are being burned off. People can still get the same result without the burning feeling. They just need gentler exercise over a longer period.

WHAT HAPPENS IF...?

What if you do this demonstration slowly? Speed is part of the key to it all. Think back to those images of people in the gym "feeling the burn." It's usually quick-moving exercises that get that reaction. Slow, gentle exercises, such as yoga, call for stamina over the long term instead of quick, high-powered energy drains.

Hold the Line

Planting a seed and watching it grow over time can be a peaceful experience, but sometimes it's hard to be patient! It might seem hard to tell whether the plant is growing healthily when it's only growing a few millimeters each day. Is there an easier way of monitoring plant growth? Yes—and you can try it yourself!

YOU WILL NEED

- 1 bean seed
- Small flowerpot
- Potting soil or compost
- 16 inches (40 cm) of cotton thread
- Plastic straw
- Drawing pin
- Card stock
- 2 heavy books
- Water
- Pen

1

Soak the bean seed in water overnight, then plant it in the flowerpot filled with soil or compost.

2

Line the two books up next to the flowerpot and stand the card between them, so that it's upright. Press the books together to keep it firm.

3

Tie the thread to one end of the straw.

4

Stick the pin through the middle of the straw and pin it to the card. The pin should be about 6 inches (15 cm) higher than the top of the flowerpot and 6 inches (15 cm) in from the card edge nearest to the flowerpot.

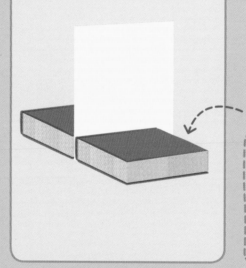

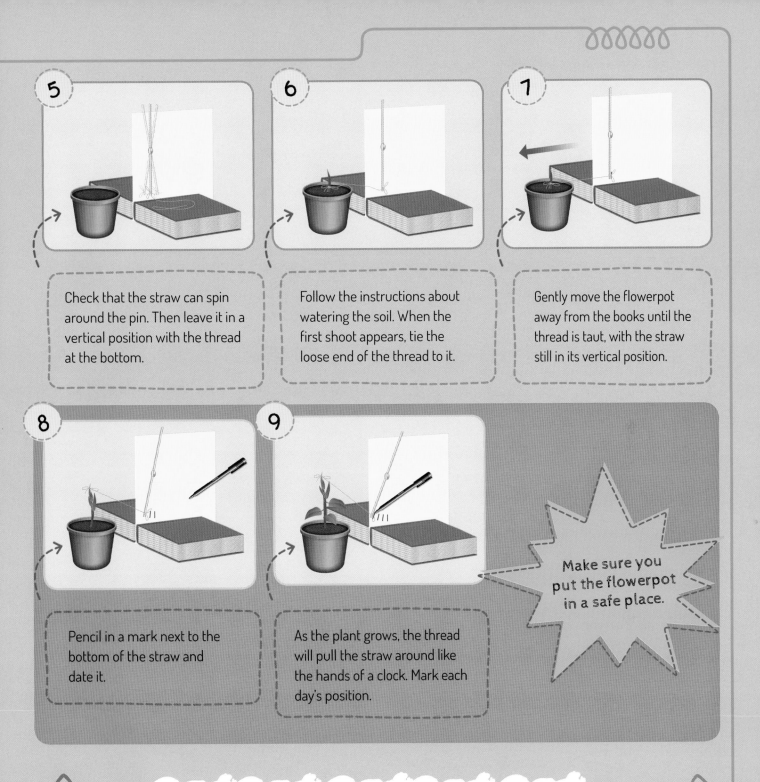

5 Check that the straw can spin around the pin. Then leave it in a vertical position with the thread at the bottom.

6 Follow the instructions about watering the soil. When the first shoot appears, tie the loose end of the thread to it.

7 Gently move the flowerpot away from the books until the thread is taut, with the straw still in its vertical position.

8 Pencil in a mark next to the bottom of the straw and date it.

9 As the plant grows, the thread will pull the straw around like the hands of a clock. Mark each day's position.

Make sure you put the flowerpot in a safe place.

TOP TIP!

If you can manage it, try piercing the end of the straw with the pin point, and looping the thread through the small hole — there's less chance of the thread slipping off that way.

Continued

HOW DOES IT WORK?

This experiment depends on the bean growing more than anything else. You've given it the ideal conditions to prepare for growth. Soaking the seed triggers a mechanism that tells the seed there's enough moisture to **germinate**, or begin to grow. The soil or compost, coupled with regular watering and sunlight, help to provide perfect growing conditions. Once the seedling has popped out, it begins to tug the thread upwards. This movement is translated into the curved motion of the straw. Scientists and engineers describe a **force** that causes a rotation as "torque." It's the same force that turns a car's axle, but you've used it to power the straw!

WHAT HAPPENS IF...?

You can change some of the **variables** of this experiment to see if you get different results. You could compare the growth of different seeds. You could even predict whether a seed would grow faster or higher than the bean based on a change you made.

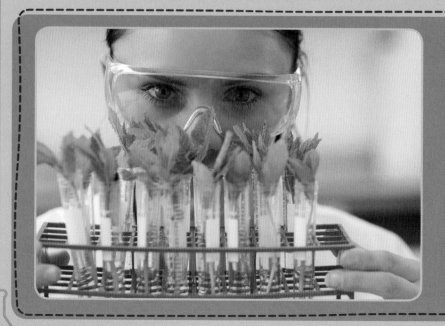

REAL-LIFE SCIENCE

Agriculture is the scientific term for growing healthy plants—often as quickly as possible. Scientists and farmers are constantly looking for plant types known as strains that grow the best in difficult conditions. They can even make money by selling the seeds of their best-performing plants.

Stop That Landslide!

Landslides occur when the ground on a slope is unstable. They're dramatic and often destructive. Some of the same conditions lead to the less sensational but equally destructive effects of soil erosion. Could plants come to the rescue?

YOU WILL NEED

- 2 plastic seed trays, each about 9 × 7 × 2 inch (230 × 170 × 50 mm)
- 2 identical high-sided baking trays, larger than the seed trays
- Soil from your garden or potting soil
- Radish seeds
- Kitchen scales
- Ruler
- Water
- Watering can
- Paper and pencil
- Scissors
- 2 ice cube trays

1

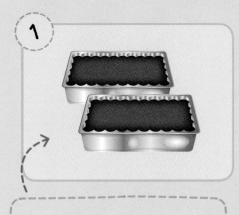

Fill each seed tray almost to the top with soil. Leave ½ inch (1 cm) at the top.

2

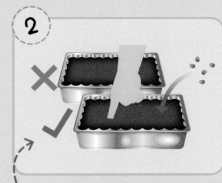

Plant radish seeds in one of the trays, following the instructions, but putting them closer together than suggested.

3

Weigh one of the baking trays using the kitchen scale and record the weight.

4

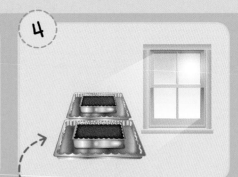

Put each seed tray on a baking tray and place them side by side in a sunny spot — inside or out (as long as the weather is warm enough).

5

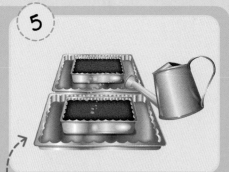

Water each tray carefully once a day for the next seven days.

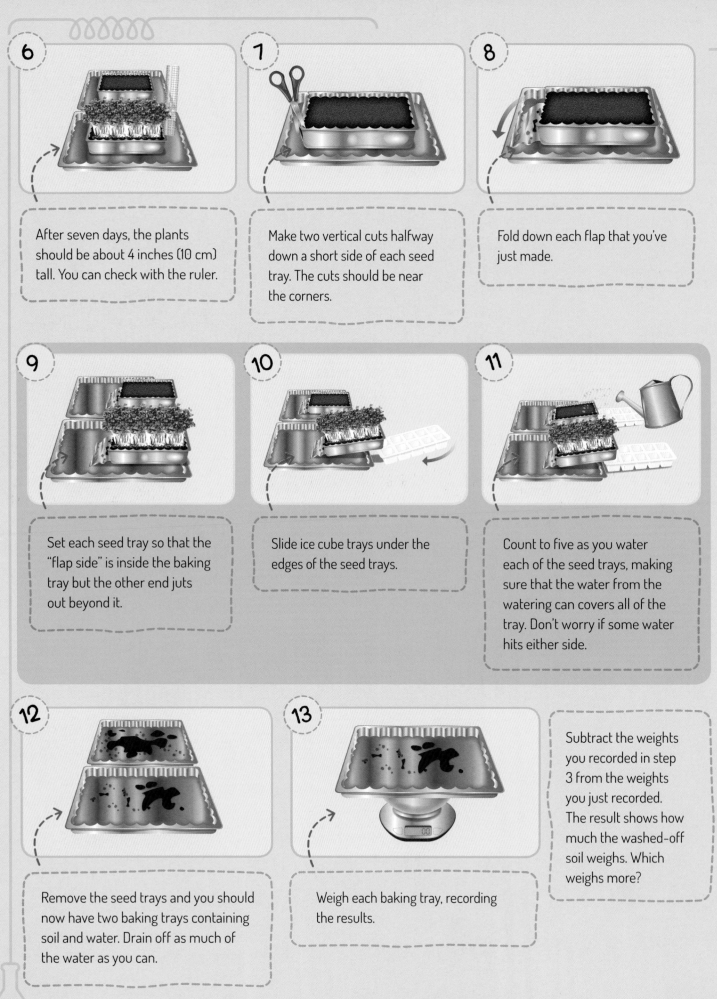

6

After seven days, the plants should be about 4 inches (10 cm) tall. You can check with the ruler.

7

Make two vertical cuts halfway down a short side of each seed tray. The cuts should be near the corners.

8

Fold down each flap that you've just made.

9

Set each seed tray so that the "flap side" is inside the baking tray but the other end juts out beyond it.

10

Slide ice cube trays under the edges of the seed trays.

11

Count to five as you water each of the seed trays, making sure that the water from the watering can covers all of the tray. Don't worry if some water hits either side.

12

Remove the seed trays and you should now have two baking trays containing soil and water. Drain off as much of the water as you can.

13

Weigh each baking tray, recording the results.

Subtract the weights you recorded in step 3 from the weights you just recorded. The result shows how much the washed-off soil weighs. Which weighs more?

HOW DOES IT WORK?

In this experiment, your baking trays are like miniature "hillsides." You've measured how much soil runs off with "rain." That's a huge cause of soil erosion. Plant roots act as anchors, causing the soil to clump together and resist being washed away. Maybe you've seen how soil sticks to the roots of plants and weeds that you pull up. You ignored the instructions about spacing the plants because this experiment is about those roots, and you want the crowded seeds to produce a tangle of roots. You can thin the plants out for better growth after the experiment.

TOP TIP!

Remember that you're trying to reproduce the effects of rain, which falls evenly over the ground. Hold the watering can high enough to "rain" on the trays evenly.

WHAT HAPPENS IF...?

You can become really scientific by testing how effective different plants are. You'll need more time, and a few more baking trays! You could do several tests at once, trying different types of seeds.

REAL-LIFE SCIENCE

Many parts of the world have lost valuable farming land because of soil erosion. Anchoring the soil with plants is an excellent way of protecting against heavy seasonal rains, which cause so much damage. "Plant anchors" can even work in sand. Many coastal areas are planted with types of beach grass to protect the dunes.

Making Breakfast

Live! From your kitchen! We bring you some breakfast yogurt! Actually, YOU'LL be bringing the yogurt once you've done this experiment. Before long, you'll see why the word "live" is so important. **Bacteria** never tasted so good.

1 Scoop out 4 tablespoons of yogurt into a bowl.

2 Warm the bowl in a microwave for about 2 minutes, until it's 107 – 111 °F (42 – 44 °C).

3 Add a tablespoon of yogurt to the second bowl. Now stir 4 tablespoons of warm milk into that second bowl.

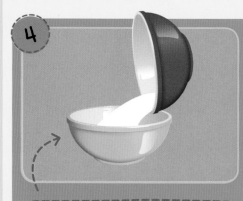

4 Add the yogurt and milk mixture into the first bowl. Stir it well and spread it evenly.

5 Cover the bowl with a tea towel and put it back in the microwave. Shut the door to keep the heat in, but do not turn it on.

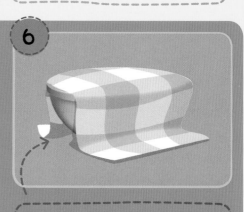

6 Leave for 10 – 12 hours and uncover. You should have thick, delicious yogurt!

HOW DOES IT WORK?

This experiment is all about bacteria. These tiny organisms eat the lactose (a type of sugar) in the milk to gain energy and to reproduce. Lactic acid is produced as a result, and these acid **molecules** react with the protein in the milk. Those protein molecules, in turn, get reshaped so that they stick together. The "sticking together" quality is what we recognize as yogurt. "Live" yogurt means that it contains the bacteria that will be needed to start the process. As you saw, you only need a little yogurt from one batch to turn a much larger amount of milk into more yogurt!

TOP TIP!

Remember — this experiment only works with live yogurt, preferably bought on the same day.

REAL-LIFE SCIENCE

No one knows for sure who first discovered yogurt, but many people believe that it was in the Asian region of Mesopotamia (modern Iraq) more than 5,000 years ago. It might even have been an accident — some goat's milk might have turned to yogurt in the warm conditions.

WHAT HAPPENS IF...?

Like many science experiments, you can learn a lot from this demonstration even if it doesn't turn out how you expected. Do you think this experiment would still work with regular yogurt? Why or why not?

How Tall is that Tree?

YOU WILL NEED

- Measuring tape
- Yardstick
- Tree with open space

Imagine being able to measure the height of a tree without having to climb or touch it! You could take a guess, and you might get pretty close to the right measurement. Or you could use engineering, which ties science to practical jobs, to get a solid answer! All you need is a yardstick.

1

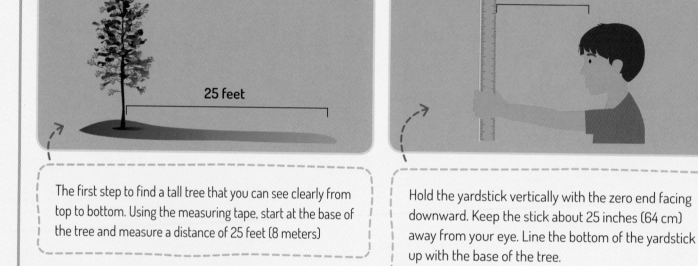

25 feet

The first step to find a tall tree that you can see clearly from top to bottom. Using the measuring tape, start at the base of the tree and measure a distance of 25 feet (8 meters)

2

25 inches

Hold the yardstick vertically with the zero end facing downward. Keep the stick about 25 inches (64 cm) away from your eye. Line the bottom of the yardstick up with the base of the tree.

3

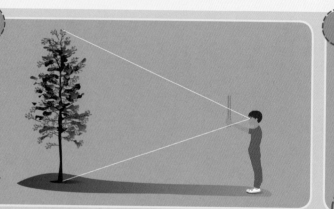

Without moving your head, look to see where the top of the tree lines up with the yardstick. Each inch equals 1 foot of height (10 cm equals 1 m of height), so now you know how tall the tree is!

4

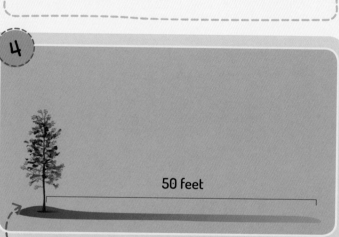

50 feet

If you couldn't see the top of the tree line up with the yardstick from 25 feet, try again from 50 feet (15 m) away. Multiply the measurement by 2 to find the height of the tree.

HOW DOES IT WORK?

You've created an engineering tool called a hypsometer, a device to calculate height or altitude. Engineering is where science and mathematics meet—this experiment uses triangulation to work out the height. As you might expect, triangulation involves triangles. You had two triangles in this experiment, one being a mini-version of the other. The big imaginary triangle's sides were the connection between your eye and the top of the tree, your eye and the bottom of the tree, and the tree trunk. The small imaginary triangle was formed by the connection between your eye and top of the tree, your eye and the bottom of the tree, and the yardstick.

TOP TIP!

A tree in a park or someone's yard is ideal, because your view of it isn't blocked by other trees or vegetation.

WHAT HAPPENS IF...?

What if walking 50 feet (15 m) away from the tree still isn't enough? You can walk out 75 feet (23 m) and multiply your measurement by 3 to find the height of your extremely tall tree!

REAL-LIFE SCIENCE

Not all hypsometers use triangulation to work out height or altitude. Some measure the temperature at which water boils to calculate altitude. The higher the altitude, the lower the temperature at which water boils. This means it would take longer to boil water on a mountain than on a beach! Precise measurements of height or altitude can help with forest regeneration, tree surgery, and plant studies.

A Matter of Taste

YOU WILL NEED

- Apple
- Pear (not too ripe—it should feel a bit like an apple)
- Sharp knife
- Vanilla essence
- 2 small plates
- Cotton balls
- 2 or 3 friends and an adult to help you
- Blindfold (optional)

Question: What's the difference between an apple and a pear? **Answer:** Only your nose knows! This simple experiment will have your friends wondering what's gone wrong with their taste buds. You'll all be surprised by how easy it is to trick your sense of taste.

1 Ask an adult to help you cut the apple and pear into about eight pieces each and set the pieces on the two plates. Make sure you know which plate has which fruit.

2 Ask your friends to line up and close their eyes or use blindfolds. Give each of them a slice of fruit. Ask them to taste it and identify it. They'll get it right — this time!

3 Put a few drops of vanilla essence onto cotton balls and give one to each friend.

4 Now get them to hold the cotton ball under their nose and close their eyes.

5 Give them another piece of fruit while they are smelling the vanilla, and see how well they identify it. It's much harder now! Continue until you run out of fruit.

HOW DOES IT WORK?

This experiment shows how closely the sense of taste is linked to the sense of smell. Your tongue has special sensors called taste buds to tell your brain about the food you're eating. But they can only pass on information about five basic tastes—sweet, sour, salty, bitter, and umami (a meaty flavor).

The rest of what you "taste" comes from what your nose picks up as smells. And in this case, the strong smell of vanilla overpowered the tastes of either fruit. Maybe that's why small children hold their noses when they have to eat vegetables!

TOP TIPS!

Make sure an adult uses the sharp knife to cut up the fruit.

REAL-LIFE SCIENCE

There are many foods and drinks that smell better than they taste—or taste better than they smell! Many people love the smell of fresh coffee but don't like the taste of the drink. And in parts of Asia, a fruit known as durian can't be displayed in open-air markets because it smells so bad—but some people say that it tastes delicious!

WHAT HAPPENS IF...?

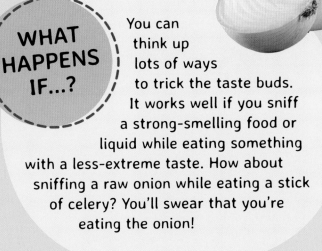

You can think up lots of ways to trick the taste buds. It works well if you sniff a strong-smelling food or liquid while eating something with a less-extreme taste. How about sniffing a raw onion while eating a stick of celery? You'll swear that you're eating the onion!

The Drooling Plant

That sounds a bit disgusting, doesn't it? Would it be any better if this experiment had been called "The Peeing Plant"? It could have been! A lot of substances go in and out of plants all the time. You just need to know how to look.

1

Set a healthy houseplant near a sunny window. Find a strong stem with a large leaf or a cluster of leaves.

2

Slide the sandwich bag over the leaf or cluster so that the mouth of the bag is close to the stem. Make sure the bag doesn't crush the plant.

3

Carefully secure the mouth of the bag with tape. You don't have to make it very tight—a little gap won't matter.

4

After two hours, remove the bag and examine it. You'll see drops of water lining the inside.

5

Repeat this experiment on the same leaves or cluster with a new bag, but water the plant well before you leave it. See whether the second bag collects more water.

HOW DOES IT WORK?

This experiment is all about the way that plants can "suck" water up from the soil and carry it all the way to their outermost leaves. Along the way, the plant is able to use minerals that are dissolved in the water. This process is called transpiration. When water reaches the end of the line, it evaporates from tiny holes in the plant's leaves. But at the same time, the plant is sucking in more water, so the process continues. The rate of transpiration sometimes increases if there's more water to be found. You might have found the same thing in the last step of this experiment, when you increased the water supply!

H_2O

H_2O

REAL-LIFE SCIENCE

Not every plant can afford to lose water so easily. Plants in deserts, for example, can't waste precious water by letting it evaporate. That's why cactus plants and other desert-natives have such small leaves. The smaller the leaf, the less it allows water to escape through evaporation.

WHAT HAPPENS IF...?

You don't have to limit yourself to houseplants. Try placing a plastic bag on some low tree branches. You could compare how much water each type of tree produces.

Plant Breath

We all know that plants need water, sunlight, and some gases (especially carbon dioxide) from the air to produce food. We also know they get rid of oxygen as waste. But wouldn't it be fun to witness this process as it happens? Here's how you can!

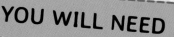

YOU WILL NEED

- 2 drinking glasses
- 2 green leaves from a tree or bush that are almost as big as the mouths of the glasses
- Water
- Magnifying glass
- Sunny windowsill and dark closet or cupboard

1

Make sure you've chosen leaves of about the same size. Test each to make sure it will fit in the glass without bending. Fill the two glasses almost to the top with water.

2

Rest a leaf on the water of each glass.

3

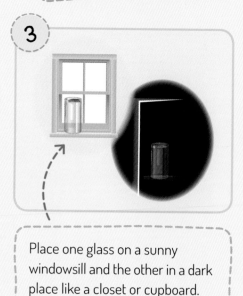

Place one glass on a sunny windowsill and the other in a dark place like a closet or cupboard.

4

Wait one hour and then compare both glasses. Look for bubbles on the edge of the leaves and on the glasses themselves. Try looking even more closely with a magnifying glass to see the tiniest bubbles.

5

Return the glasses to the windowsill and dark area for another hour. See whether there are more bubbles.

HOW DOES IT WORK?

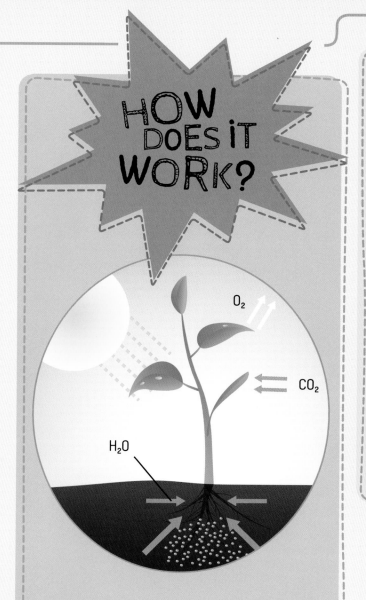

O₂

CO₂

H₂O

The bubbles you observed were oxygen, the waste given off by plants after they have created their own food through a process called **photosynthesis**. That long word comes from two Greek words—photo (meaning "light") and synthesis (meaning "making"). And that's exactly what plants do—they make food from light.

Since plants need light to make food, the leaf kept in the dark wasn't able to make much food. How do we know? Making more food would mean producing more waste. The glass in the sunny spot contained many more bubbles of oxygen, or waste!

REAL-LIFE SCIENCE

You can sometimes see a difference in leaves on the same tree. Those nearest the top of the tree—with more exposure to light—usually look greener and healthier than those below, which are shaded from the direct light. You'd probably see more oxygen bubbles coming from those higher leaves for the same reason.

WHAT HAPPENS IF...?

If you picked a leaf and left it in the sun for an hour before placing it in water, you'd see very few bubbles. The leaf would be dead, so you might not see any bubbles at all. Water is important not just in making food, but in helping the food spread within a plant.

The Bouncing Egg

Fried, poached, and scrambled eggs are all tasty, but would you ever order a bouncing egg for breakfast? It might not be your first choice, but it's a lot more fun to play with. Just don't eat the results of this crazy recipe!

YOU WILL NEED

- An uncooked egg
- Vinegar
- Old drinking glass, at least "2 eggs high" inside
- Paper towel
- Spoon

1

Tilt the glass and carefully put the egg inside it.

2

Stand the glass upright and pour in enough vinegar to cover the egg completely. You'll start to see some bubbles emerging from the shell.

3

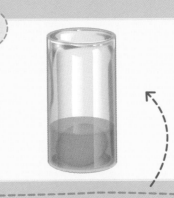

Leave the egg in the glass for four days, but observe it regularly to note changes in the shell. The bubbling will stop when the shell has dissolved.

4

Tilt the glass a little over a sink and gently remove the egg, using the spoon. Lay the egg on two pieces of paper towel to let the vinegar drain off its surface. The shell will have disappeared, replaced with a waxy coating.

5

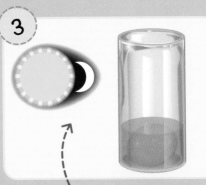

You can hold the egg carefully and it won't burst. Try dropping it from a low height, about 2 inches (5 cm). See how high you can go before things get very messy!

26

HOW DOES IT WORK?

You've just used a chemical reaction to work a little magic. Eggshells contain calcium, a chemical element that gives them their hardness. Your bones are hard because they also have lots of calcium.

Vinegar contains a substance called acetic acid, which reacts with the calcium of the eggshell. That reaction produces the gas called carbon dioxide (those were the bubbles), and it uses up the calcium along the way. What's left is called the egg membrane, the almost transparent and flexible covering of the egg.

REAL-LIFE SCIENCE

Many rocks in the ground are made up of calcium carbonate, the same as eggshells. As rain seeps through the rock, the calcium carbonate is dissolved. That's because the water contains small amounts of acid. Sometimes the water reaches a cave, and the air in the cave reverses the process. The calcium carbonate reappears as towering stalactites and stalagmites.

WHAT HAPPENS IF...?

Try putting the "shell-less" egg in another glass, filling the glass with water, and leaving it in the refrigerator for 24 hours. It will become much bigger! That's because the soft membrane allows water to pass through it, "pumping up" the inside of the egg.

TOP TIPS!

Make sure that you test the egg somewhere that you can clean up easily.

Soil Tests

Did you know that there's a special type of science that deals with getting the best results from dirt? Well, not necessarily dirt, but the soil in which things are planted. But soil is soil—right? What's the big difference, anyway? You might think differently after this experiment!

1

Poke three holes in the bottom of each cup.

2

Spread a layer of potting soil across the seed tray. It should be 1 inch (2 cm) deep.

3

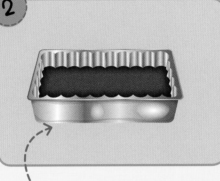

Spread about 15 sunflower seeds on the tray and cover them with another layer of potting soil. It should be about ½ inch (1 cm) thick.

4

Water the soil evenly and store the tray in a warm place.

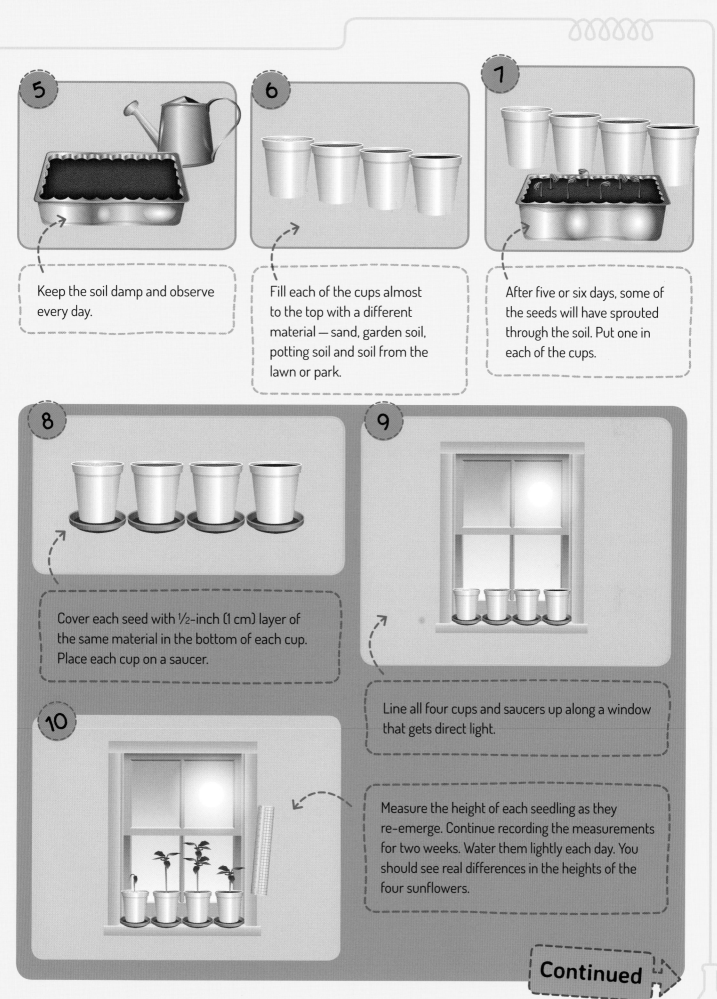

5 Keep the soil damp and observe every day.

6 Fill each of the cups almost to the top with a different material — sand, garden soil, potting soil and soil from the lawn or park.

7 After five or six days, some of the seeds will have sprouted through the soil. Put one in each of the cups.

8 Cover each seed with ½-inch (1 cm) layer of the same material in the bottom of each cup. Place each cup on a saucer.

9 Line all four cups and saucers up along a window that gets direct light.

10 Measure the height of each seedling as they re-emerge. Continue recording the measurements for two weeks. Water them lightly each day. You should see real differences in the heights of the four sunflowers.

Continued

HOW DOES IT WORK?

The first step in the experiment was to help the seeds germinate. They had all the ideal conditions at this stage—warmth, darkness, and damp soil. The real experiment was to see how well each seedling grew in the different soil conditions. Two of the main elements for growth—light and moisture—were the same for all four small plants. The difference was the material in which they were growing. In addition to light and water, plants benefit from the boost that other minerals can provide. It's a bit like the way people take vitamins in addition to the food they eat. You can judge which of the soils contained the best minerals for growth based on the plants' success.

TOP TIP!

Ask an adult to poke the holes in the cups for you.

Make sure that you keep the cups together as you monitor the growth of the plants.

WHAT HAPPENS IF...?

If you left any of the healthy plants too long in the cups, they'd become "pot-bound," meaning that their roots lacked enough room to grow properly. At that stage, you can "re-pot" them into something larger and eventually plant them outside in a sunny patch of your backyard.

REAL-LIFE SCIENCE

Agronomy is the branch of science that deals with crops and soil, and it's very important. You've just seen how some types of soil are more productive than others. Imagine trying to find the best conditions to grow crops for a whole country! That's why agronomists are so important.

Glossary

bacteria Tiny one-celled organisms.

calorie A unit of energy.

cell The smallest part of an organism.

energy The power or ability to do work such as moving. Energy can be transferred from one object to another, but it cannot be destroyed.

force The strength of a particular energy at work.

germinate Begin to grow.

molecule The smallest unit of a substance, such as oxygen, that has all the properties of that substance.

nutrient A substance that helps plants and animals to live and grow.

oxygen A colorless gas with no smell, all organisms need oxygen to live.

photosynthesis The process that allows plants to use sunlight to change water and carbon dioxide into food for itself.

prediction A guess about what will happen in the future as a result of an action.

unique Something that is one of a kind, not like anything else.

variable A part of an experiment that can change.

Further Information

Books to read

100 Steps for Science: Why it works and how it happened by Lisa Jane Gillespie and Yukai Du (Wide Eyed Editions, 2017)

Mind Webs: Living Things by Anna Claybourne (Wayland, 2017)

Whizzy Science: Make it Grow by Anna Claybourne (Wayland, 2014)

Websites

https://www.education.com/activity/plants-animals-the-earth/
Check out this amazing site for more incredible experiments with plants, animals, and Earth science.

http://climatekids.nasa.gov/menu/plants-and-animals/
Visit NASA's awesome website on climate change and living things for kids.

http://www.dkfindout.com/us/animals-and-nature/
Explore this interactive website for fascinating facts on living things!

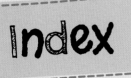

Index